The Mermaid Parade

Kelly Doudna

Consulting Editor, Diane Craig, M.A./Reading Specialist

ABDO
Publishing Company

Published by ABDO Publishing Company, 4940 Viking Drive, Edina, Minnesota 55435.

Printed in the United States.

Credits
Edited by: Pam Price
Curriculum Coordinator: Nancy Tuminelly
Cover and Interior Design and Production: Mighty Media
Photo Credits: BananaStock Ltd., Brand X Pictures, Corbis Images, Eyewire Imges, Hemera, Image 100, Image Source, ImageState, PhotoDisc, Rubberball Productions

Library of Congress Cataloging-in-Publication Data

Doudna, Kelly, 1963-
     The mermaid parade / Kelly Doudna.
        p. cm. -- (Rhyme time)
     ISBN 1-59197-804-1 (hardcover)
     ISBN 1-59197-910-2 (paperback)
     1. English language--Rhyme--Juvenile literature. I. Title. II. Rhyme time (ABDO Publishing Company)

PE1517.D686 2004
428.1'3--dc22
                                                                    2004047350

SandCastle™ books are created by a professional team of educators, reading specialists, and content developers around five essential components that include phonemic awareness, phonics, vocabulary, text comprehension, and fluency. All books are written, reviewed, and leveled for guided reading, early intervention reading, and Accelerated Reader® programs and designed for use in shared, guided, and independent reading and writing activities to support a balanced approach to literacy instruction.

Let Us Know

After reading the book, SandCastle would like you to tell us your stories about reading. What is your favorite page? Was there something hard that you needed help with? Share the ups and downs of learning to read. We want to hear from you! To get posted on the ABDO Publishing Company Web site, send us e-mail at:

sandcastle@abdopub.com

SandCastle Level: Fluent

Words that rhyme do not have to be spelled the same. These words rhyme with each other:

afraid

lemonade

braid

maid

glade

parade

grade

raid

laid

shade

When Frankie goes to the dentist, he is not **afraid**.

Vicky, Ryan, and their parents have a picnic in a **glade**.

Tara has red beads on the end of each braid.

David does his homework so he will get a good grade.

It was Sue's job to make sure the table was laid.

Marie and Carolyn are selling
lemonade.

Kate and Toni don't like to wash dishes.

They wish they had a **maid**.

Hundreds of people came to watch the **parade**.

Paul is sending his toy soldiers on a secret raid.

Beth and Zach sit in the **shade** under the umbrella.

The Mermaid Parade

The people in Cascade became afraid
that the summer would pass
without a parade.

So a meeting was held,
and they served lemonade.
Plans were laid
to stage the parade.

Jade with the braid
asked, "Who will we persuade
to be in our parade?"

16

They were dismayed
by the dunce
who didn't make the grade.

The warrior was away
on a crusade.

He was in the middle
of an important raid.

Mr. Wade was too busy
painting in the glade.

That is where he stayed.

At last they spied a mermaid,
who was resting in the shade.

Jade cried, "This is the plan that will be okayed.

We're going to have a mermaid parade!"

Rhyming Riddle

What do you call a housekeeper's report card?

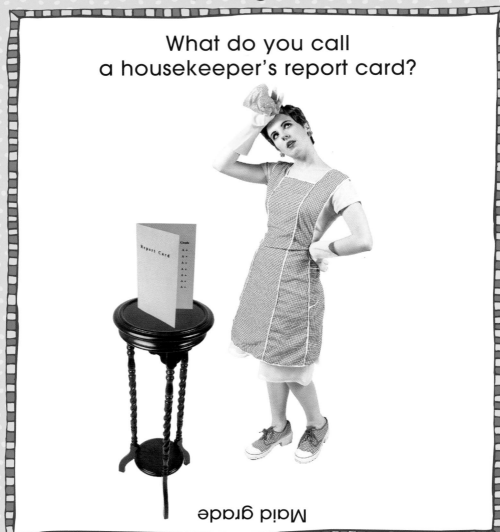

Maid grade

Glossary

crusade. a vigorous battle or fight for or against something

glade. a grassy, open space inside a forest

mermaid. a fictional creature with the upper body of a woman and the tail of a fish

parade. a public procession held in celebration

raid. a surprise attack by a small military group

About SandCastle™

A professional team of educators, reading specialists, and content developers created the SandCastle™ series to support young readers as they develop reading skills and strategies and increase their general knowledge. The SandCastle™ series has four levels that correspond to early literacy development in young children. The levels are provided to help teachers and parents select the appropriate books for young readers.

Emerging Readers
(no flags)

Beginning Readers
(1 flag)

Transitional Readers
(2 flags)

Fluent Readers
(3 flags)

These levels are meant only as a guide. All levels are subject to change.

To see a complete list of SandCastle™ books and other nonfiction titles from ABDO Publishing Company, visit www.abdopub.com or contact us at:
4940 Viking Drive, Edina, Minnesota 55435 • 1-800-800-1312 • fax: 1-952-831-1632